Collections for Young Scholars™

EXPLORER'S NOTEBOOK

VOLUME 2

PROGRAM AUTHORS
Carl Bereiter
Valerie Anderson
Ann Brown
Marlene Scardamalia
Joe Campione

CONSULTING AUTHORS
Michael Pressley
Iva Carruthers
Bill Pinkney

OPEN COURT PUBLISHING COMPANY
CHICAGO AND PERU, ILLINOIS

Cover art by Kate Keller
Interior art by Jan Adkins, Tony Caldwell, Fran Lee, Michael McCurdy,
Lynne Titleman, Joyce Audy Zarins
Composition and elctronic page makeup were provided by Itzhack Shelomi Design

Knowledge About Being Brave

This is what I know about being brave before reading the unit.

_____

_____

_____

_____

_____

_____

These are some things I would like to know about being brave.

_____

_____

_____

_____

_____

_____

Reminder: I should read this page again when I get
to the end of the unit to see how much I've learned
about being brave.

Recording Concept Information

As I read each story, this is what I found out about being brave.

"Dragons and Giants" by Arnold Lobel

_____

_____

_____

_____

_____

_____

The Hole in the Dike, retold by Norma Green

_____

_____

_____

_____

_____

_____

_____

Molly the Brave and Me by Jane O'Connor

_____

_____

_____

_____

_____

_____

_____

The Legend of the Bluebonnet, retold by Tomie dePaola

_____

_____

_____

_____

_____

_____

_____

_____

Recording Concept Information continued

Sally Ride, Astronaut: An American First by June Behrens

_____

_____

_____

_____

_____

_____

_____

_____

_____

_____

Bravery on the Job

Can you think of some jobs that brave people might do? When would a person in one of these jobs need to be brave? Why? Write your ideas below. Share and talk about your ideas with your classmates. Add to your ideas as you read and learn more about being brave.

Job	When and How to Be Brave
_____	_____
	_____
	_____
_____	_____
	_____
	_____
_____	_____
	_____
	_____
_____	_____
	_____
	_____

Being Brave: Who? What? Why?

What do you think makes someone brave? Why? Write down ideas. Then talk about them with your classmates.

_____

_____

_____

_____

_____

_____

_____

_____

Do you know of anyone who has shown that he or she is brave? What did this person do? Share what you know with your classmates.

_____

_____

_____

_____

_____

_____

_____

_____

Would you like to be brave in some way? What would you have to do?
Write about it here.

_____

_____

_____

_____

_____

_____

_____

_____

Do you have any more questions about being brave? If so, write them
here.

_____

_____

_____

_____

_____

_____

_____

_____

Collecting Information

Ask your family and friends what people need to be brave about and when they need to be brave. Find out what they think and ask them to give examples of their ideas.

Write down the information you find. Use the headings below to help you. List the things people talked about next to the correct headings. Add new headings, if you like. Add to the list as you read through the unit.

Friends	**What? When? Why?**
At School	_____
	_____
	_____
	_____
At Play	_____
	_____
	_____
	_____
In the Community	_____
	_____
	_____
	_____

Adults	What? When? Why?
At School	_____
	_____
	_____
	_____
In the Community	_____
	_____
	_____
	_____
Other	_____
	_____
	_____
	_____

Notes: _____

_____

_____

_____

_____

_____

_____

Recording Questions

What would you like to explore about being brave? Write your questions or ideas here.

_____
_____
_____
_____
_____
_____
_____
_____
_____
_____
_____

What books might you read to find answers to your questions?

_____
_____
_____
_____
_____
_____
_____
_____

Planning Exploration

How can you further explore being brave? You may have already started asking questions to find out when people need to be brave and what they need to be brave about. What else can you ask?

Find out what people think "being brave" means.

_____

_____

_____

_____

As you begin your exploration of being brave, you will want to keep a list of things you need to do. Check off each item as you finish it. Here is the start of a list of things you might want to do. Add to it as you read the unit.

Things to Do

☐ Talk to friends

☐ Talk to adults

☐ Find and use books from bibliographies

☐ _____

☐ _____

☐ _____

Interview

Many people have been brave at one time or another. Talk to someone about his or her experience with being brave. Ask that person what the problem was and what she or he did to solve it. Share this information with your classmates.

Problem: _____

_____

_____

_____

_____

_____

How the person solved the problem: _____

_____

_____

_____

_____

_____

Why this was brave: _____

_____

_____

_____

Famous Brave People

Find out about people who were brave and became famous for their bravery. Check newspapers, magazines, and books. List the people's names and what they did that was brave on the chart below. The first line has been filled in as an example. Compare your lists with those of your classmates. Share your ideas about why each person on your list was brave.

You may wish to pick one of the people from your list and make a photo essay about that person's life. Find pictures from newspapers and magazine articles or draw your own pictures of important times in the brave person's life, based on what you have read.

Name	What she/he did
Sally Ride	First American woman astronaut in space

Qualities of a Brave Person

From your reading you have learned that being unselfish is one way of being brave. Find out what other qualities a brave person is expected to have. Look through books, magazines, and newspapers or ask people what qualities they expect to find in a brave person. List the qualities and tell why these qualities are important.

Qualities of a Brave Person   **Explain**

Qualities of a Brave Person   **Explain**

You may wish to pick one of the qualities that a brave person would have and draw a picture to show it. For example, if you think that honesty is a quality of a brave person, draw a picture that comes to mind when you think about a person who is being honest.

Unit Wrap-up

How did you feel about this unit?

- ☐ I enjoyed it very much.
- ☐ I liked it.
- ☐ I liked some of it.
- ☐ I didn't like it.

How would you rate the difficulty of the unit?

- ☐ easy ☐ medium ☐ hard

How would you rate your performance during this unit?

- ☐ I learned a lot about being brave.
- ☐ I learned some things about being brave.
- ☐ I didn't learn much about being brave.

Why did you choose this rating?

_____

_____

_____

_____

_____

What was the most interesting thing that you learned about being brave?

_____

_____

_____

_____

_____

What did you learn about being brave that you didn't know before?

_____

_____

_____

What did you learn about yourself as a learner?

_____

_____

_____

What do you need to work on as a learner?

_____

_____

_____

What resources (books, films, magazines, interviews, tool cards, other)
did you use on your own during this unit? Which of these were the most
helpful? Why?

_____

_____

_____

_____

_____

_____

Knowledge About Being Rich and Being Poor

This is what I know about about being rich and being poor before reading the unit.

_____

_____

_____

_____

_____

_____

These are some things I would like to know about being rich and being poor.

_____

_____

_____

_____

_____

Reminder: I should read this page again when I get to the end of the unit to see how much I have learned about being rich and being poor.

Recording Concept Information

As I read each story, this is what I found out about being rich and being poor.

"The Three Wishes" by Anna Holst

_____

_____

_____

_____

_____

_____

"The Goose That Laid the Golden Eggs" by Aesop

_____

_____

_____

_____

_____

_____

Recording Concept Information *continued*

The Empty Pot by Demi

_____

_____

_____

_____

_____

_____

_____

Cinderella, retold by Fabio Coen

_____

_____

_____

_____

_____

_____

_____

_____

The Simple Prince by Jane Yolen

_____

_____

_____

_____

_____

"Amadou's Story" by Linda Robbins

_____

_____

_____

_____

_____

"The Golden Goose" by Jacob and Wilhelm Grimm

_____

_____

_____

_____

_____

Classifying Wishes

Riches	Helpful Things	Others
Totals:		

Rich and Poor/Unit 2

Ideas About Wealth

What do you think makes one person rich and another poor? What is the best way to gain wealth? Begin with "The Three Wishes" to start the idea web below. Talk with classmates, sharing ideas. Add ideas as you read the stories in the unit.

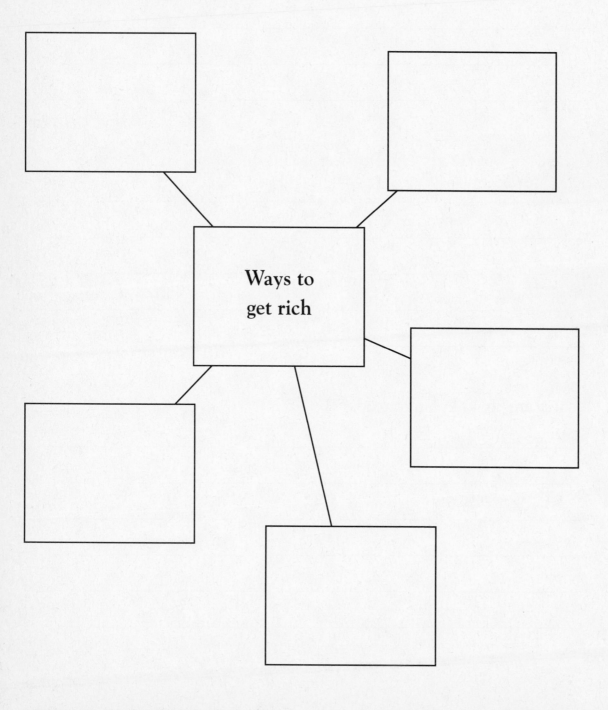

Ways to get rich

Learning About Being Rich and Being Poor

These are questions I have about being rich and being poor.

_____

_____

_____

_____

These are ways I might find answers to my questions.

_____

_____

_____

_____

These are books I plan to read.

_____

_____

_____

_____

_____

Here are answers I have found.

_____

_____

_____

_____

_____

_____

_____

_____

Here are ways I might present my findings to the class.

_____

_____

_____

_____

_____

_____

_____

_____

Making Comparisons

Advantages	Disadvantages
The Simple Life	
The Life of a Prince	

Advice to the Simple Prince

Read through the advantages and disadvantages your group listed on page 28. Then write a letter of advice to the prince on how he might put together the two lifestyles for a happier life.

Dear Prince,

_____

_____

_____

_____

_____

_____

_____

_____

_____

_____

_____

Yours truly,

Solving a Problem

Stating the Problem:

_____

_____

_____

_____

_____

Suggestions:

_____

_____

_____

_____

_____

_____

Opinions:

_____

_____

_____

_____

_____

_____

New Problems:

_____

_____

_____

_____

Suggestions:

_____

_____

_____

_____

_____

_____

Solutions:

_____

_____

_____

_____

_____

Unit Wrap-up

How did you feel about this unit?

- ☐ I enjoyed it very much.
- ☐ I liked it.
- ☐ I liked some of it.
- ☐ I didn't like it.

How would you rate the difficulty of the unit?

- ☐ easy
- ☐ medium
- ☐ hard

How would you rate your performance during this unit?

- ☐ I learned a lot about being rich and being poor.
- ☐ I learned some new things about being rich and being poor.
- ☐ I didn't learn much about being rich and being poor.

Why did you choose this rating?

_____

_____

_____

_____

What was the most interesting thing that you learned about being rich and being poor?

_____

_____

_____

_____

_____

What did you learn about being rich and being poor that you didn't know before?

_____

_____

_____

What did you learn about yourself as a learner?

_____

_____

_____

What do you need to work on as a learner?

_____

_____

_____

What resources (books, films, magazines, interviews, tool cards, other) did you use on your own during this unit? Which of these were the most helpful? Why?

_____

_____

_____

_____

Knowledge About Fossils

This is what I know about fossils before reading the unit.

_____

_____

_____

_____

_____

_____

_____

These are some things I would like to know about fossils.

_____

_____

_____

_____

_____

_____

_____

Reminder: I should read this page again when I get to the end of the unit to see how much I have learned about fossils.

Recording Concept Information

As I read each story, this is what I found out about fossils.

Fossils Tell of Long Ago by Aliki

_____

_____

_____

_____

_____

The Dinosaur Who Lived in My Backyard by B. G. Hennessy

_____

_____

_____

_____

_____

"Why Did the Dinosaurs Disappear?" by Karen Sapp

_____

_____

_____

_____

_____

Recording Concept Information *continued*

"Fossils" by Lilian Moore

_____

_____

_____

_____

"Iguanodon" by Jack Prelutsky

_____

_____

_____

_____

"Seismosaurus" by Jack Prelutsky

_____

_____

_____

_____

"Monster Tracks" by Barbara Bruno

_____

_____

_____

_____

What Do Fossils Tell?

Fossils can give clues to what life was like long, long ago. If you found a fossil, what questions would you ask about it? What might you learn from your fossil about the past?

These are the questions I would have about my fossil:

_____

_____

_____

_____

_____

_____

_____

This is what my fossil might tell me about the past:

_____

_____

_____

_____

Parts of a Book

You can find all kinds of important information in books when you know where to look. Pick one of your favorite books and use what you have learned about the parts of a book to find the following information.

Title of book: _____

_____

Author: _____

_____

Copyright date: _____

Name of a chapter from the table of contents: _____

_____

_____

Page number: _____

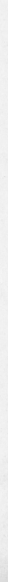

Problem Phase

A good problem for our group to research: _____

_____

_____

_____

_____

_____

Why this is an interesting research problem: _____

_____

_____

_____

_____

Some other questions about this problem: _____

_____

_____

_____

_____

_____

As you talk about the research problem with your group, the problem will change. Return to this page to record any new questions about the problem.

Living in the Days of Dinosaurs

From reading *The Dinosaur Who Lived in My Backyard*, you have learned that a dinosaur could not really fit into the human world. Would you have fit into the dinosaur's world? The questions below can help you think about it.

How I think the world looked during the time of the dinosaurs:

_____

_____

_____

_____

What I would have liked about living in the time of the dinosaurs:

_____

_____

_____

_____

What problems I would have had if I had lived in the time of the dinosaurs:

_____

_____

_____

_____

Using the Card Catalog

In the card catalog, find the titles of four books on a subject that you would like to research. Write the title, the author's name, and the location code for each book. Then on your own, or with the help of someone at the library, find these books.

Title: _____

Author's name: _____

Code: _____

Title: _____

Author's name: _____

Code: _____

Title: _____

Author's name: _____

Code: _____

Title: _____

Author's name: _____

Code: _____

Our Idea (or Conjecture) Phase

Part 1

Our research problem: _____

_____

_____

_____

My first idea or explanation: _____

_____

_____

_____

_____

_____

_____

Part 2

Our revised research problem: _____

_____

_____

_____

Our revised idea or explanation: _____

_____

_____

_____

_____

_____

_____

Going, Going . . .

You have read several theories about why dinosaurs died out, or became extinct. Today many animals are in danger of becoming extinct. That means that they are endangered. What would cause an animal to become endangered? Write your ideas below.

When do animals become endangered?

1. _____

_____

2. _____

_____

3. _____

_____

What can people do to help endangered animals?

_____

_____

_____

_____

_____

_____

_____

Table of Contents/Index

Use the table of contents and the index in books to help you find information for your research project. You can do the following:

- First, find a book on your research subject.
- Then look in the table of contents. Find a chapter that may have information that you need.
- Write the chapter title and the page number below. If you find more than one chapter with information that you need, write the title and page number of each one.
- Then look through the index of the book. Find words related to your subject.
- Write the page numbers below.

Book title: _____

Titles of chapters and page numbers with information I need:

_____

_____ Page: _____

_____

_____ Page: _____

Words related to my subject and page numbers from the index:

_____

_____ Page: _____

_____

_____ Page: _____

Track Tales

Tracks can tell many things about an animal. Write three things that you can learn by looking at an animal's tracks.

1. _____

_____

2. _____

_____

3. _____

_____

Write three things that a scientist can learn about prehistoric animals by looking at track fossils.

1. _____

_____

_____

2. _____

_____

_____

3. _____

_____

_____

Needs and Plans Phase

My group's problem:

_____

_____

Knowledge Needs—Information I need to find or figure out to help explore the problem:

A. _____

B. _____

C. _____

D. _____

E. _____

Source	Useful?	How?
Encyclopedias		
Books		
Magazines		
Newspapers		
Videotapes, filmstrips, etc.		
Television		
Interviews, observations		
Museums		
Other		

Group Plan

Our research problem:

_____

_____

_____

Group Members	Main Jobs

Unit Wrap-up

How did you feel about this unit?

☐ I enjoyed it very much.   ☐ I liked it.

☐ I liked some of it.   ☐ I didn't like it.

How would you rate the difficulty of the unit?

☐ easy   ☐ medium   ☐ hard

How would you rate your performance during this unit?

☐ I learned a lot about fossils.

☐ I learned some things about fossils.

☐ I didn't learn much about fossils.

Why did you choose this rating?

_____

_____

_____

_____

What was the most interesting thing that you learned about fossils?

_____

_____

_____

_____

_____

What did you learn about fossils that you didn't know before?

_____

_____

_____

What did you learn about yourself as a learner?

_____

_____

_____

What do you need to work on as a learner?

_____

_____

_____

What resources (books, films, magazines, interviews, tool cards, other) did you use on your own during this unit? Which of these were the most helpful? Why?

_____

_____

_____

_____

_____

Knowledge About Kindness

This is what I know about kindness before reading the unit.

_____

_____

_____

_____

_____

_____

_____

These are some things I would like to know about kindness.

_____

_____

_____

_____

_____

_____

Reminder: I should read this page again when I get to the end of the unit to see how much I have learned about kindness.

Recording Concept Information

As I read each story, this is what I found out about kindness.

The Elves and the Shoemaker, retold by Freya Littledale

_____

_____

_____

_____

_____

_____

_____

Mushroom in the Rain by Mirra Ginsburg

_____

_____

_____

_____

_____

_____

_____

Recording Concept Information *continued*

"The Camel's Nose," retold by Franco Cour

_____

_____

_____

_____

_____

_____

_____

_____

Corduroy by Don Freeman

_____

_____

_____

_____

_____

_____

_____

_____

_____

_____

Kindness/Unit 4

Clara Barton: Red Cross Pioneer by Matthew G. Grant

_____

_____

_____

_____

"The North Wind and the Sun," retold by Margaret Clark

_____

_____

_____

_____

Music, Music for Everyone by Vera B. Williams

_____

_____

_____

_____

_____

Generating Questions to Explore

These are some questions I have about kindness:

_____

_____

_____

_____

_____

_____

These are resources to help me find answers to my questions. (Remember:
People you talk to, places you visit, and magazines as well as books can be
good resources.)

_____

_____

_____

_____

_____

_____

These are books I plan to read:

_____

_____

_____

_____

_____

_____

Presenting Information

Here are answers I have found:

_____

_____

_____

_____

_____

_____

_____

These are ways I could present my new information:

_____

_____

_____

_____

_____

_____

_____

_____

_____

Setting Limits on Kindness

The man in "The Camel's Nose" was too kind for his own good. Because he was so generous, he ended up shivering out in the cold while his camel enjoyed the warmth of his tent. Has there been a time when you were too kind to someone? Write about what happened.

_____

_____

_____

_____

_____

_____

How would you (or did you) do things differently the next time?

_____

_____

_____

_____

_____

_____

Community Helpers

Many people show kindness every day in their jobs. List some jobs. You can pick jobs in the stories you are reading or any jobs that you can think of on your own. You also can list jobs that you read about in other books. Then tell how people in these jobs help others with their kindness.

Job Title	How This Person Helps Other People Through His or Her Kindness

Unit Wrap-up

How did you feel about this unit?

- ☐ I enjoyed it very much.
- ☐ I liked it.
- ☐ I liked some of it.
- ☐ I didn't like it.

How would you rate the difficulty of the unit?

- ☐ easy
- ☐ medium
- ☐ hard

How would you rate your performance during this unit?

- ☐ I learned a lot about kindness.
- ☐ I learned some things about kindness.
- ☐ I didn't learn much about kindness.

Why did you choose this rating?

_____

_____

_____

_____

What was the most interesting thing that you learned about kindness?

_____

_____

_____

_____

_____

What did you learn about kindness that you didn't know before?

_____

_____

_____

What did you learn about yourself as a learner?

_____

_____

_____

What do you need to work on as a learner?

_____

_____

_____

What resources (books, films, magazines, interviews, tool cards, other) did you use on your own during this unit? Which of these were the most helpful? Why?

_____

_____

_____

_____

_____

Knowledge About Responsibility

This is what I know about responsibility before reading the unit.

_____

_____

_____

_____

_____

_____

_____

These are some things I would like to know about responsibility.

_____

_____

_____

_____

_____

_____

_____

Reminder: I should read this page again when I get to the end of the unit to see how much I have learned about responsibility.

Recording Concept Information

As I read each story, this is what I found out about responsibility.

A *Pair of Red Clogs* by Masako Matsuno

_____

_____

_____

_____

"The Pudding Like a Night on the Sea" by Ann Cameron

_____

_____

_____

_____

"The Boy Who Cried Wolf," retold by Margaret Clark

_____

_____

_____

_____

Recording Concept Information *continued*

The Tale of Peter Rabbit by Beatrix Potter

_____

_____

_____

_____

_____

"Three Hundred Spartans" by Sonia Bradoz

_____

_____

_____

_____

"The Grasshopper and the Ants," retold by Margaret Clark

_____

_____

_____

_____

Defining Responsibility

What is responsibility? Find out what friends and classmates think. Play the Dictionary game and record the information you gather on the lines below.

_____

_____

_____

_____

_____

_____

_____

_____

_____

_____

_____

_____

_____

_____

_____

_____

_____

Learning About Responsibility

These are questions I have about responsibility:

_____

_____

_____

_____

_____

_____

_____

These are ways I might find answers to my questions:

_____

_____

_____

_____

_____

_____

_____

_____

_____

These are books I plan to read:

_____

_____

_____

_____

_____

_____

_____

_____

Here are answers I have found:

_____

_____

_____

_____

_____

_____

_____

_____

Unit 5/Responsibility

Growing in Responsibility

Complete the chart as you read through the unit.
The first selection has been done for you.

Responsibility	How Fulfilled or Ignored	Consequences
A Pair of Red Clogs		
To take care of own things	*Cracked and dirtied her clogs*	*Had to wear dirty clogs* *Guilty feelings*
"The Pudding Like a Night on the Sea"		
"The Boy Who Cried Wolf"		

Responsibility	How Fulfilled or Ignored	Consequences
The Tale of Peter Rabbit		
"Three Hundred Spartans"		
"The Grasshopper and the Ants"		

Unit Wrap-up

How did you feel about this unit?

☐ I enjoyed it very much.   ☐ I liked it.

☐ I liked some of it.   ☐ I didn't like it.

How would you rate the difficulty of the unit?

☐ easy   ☐ medium   ☐ hard

How would you rate your performance during this unit?

☐ I learned a lot about responsibility.

☐ I learned some things about responsibility.

☐ I didn't learn much about responsibility.

Why did you choose this rating?

_____

_____

_____

_____

What was the most interesting thing that you learned about responsibility?

_____

_____

_____

_____

What did you learn about responsibility that you didn't know before?

_____

_____

_____

What did you learn about yourself as a learner?

_____

_____

_____

What do you need to work on as a learner?

_____

_____

_____

What resources (books, films, magazines, interviews, tool cards, other)
did you use on your own during this unit? Which of these were the most
helpful? Why?

_____

_____

_____

_____

Knowledge About Appearances

This is what I know about appearances before reading the unit.

_____

_____

_____

_____

_____

_____

_____

These are some things I would like to know about appearances.

_____

_____

_____

_____

_____

_____

_____

Reminder: I should read this page again when I get
to the end of the unit to see how much I have learned
about appearances.

Recording Concept Information

As I read each story, this is what I learned about appearances.

Crow Boy by Taro Yashima

_____

_____

_____

_____

_____

_____

_____

"The Foolish, Timid Rabbit," retold by Ellen C. Babbitt

_____

_____

_____

_____

_____

_____

_____

_____

Recording Concept Information continued

How We Learned the Earth Is Round by Patricia Lauber

_____

_____

_____

_____

_____

"The Fox and the Crow," retold by Margaret Clark

_____

_____

_____

_____

_____

"Who Has Seen the Wind?" by Christina Rossetti

_____

_____

_____

_____

_____

"An Emerald Is as Green as Grass" by Christina Rossetti

_____

_____

_____

_____

_____

_____

"Waking" by Lilian Moore

_____

_____

_____

_____

_____

_____

The Emperor's New Clothes by Hans Christian Andersen

_____

_____

_____

_____

_____

_____

Learning About Appearances

These are questions I have about appearances:

_____

_____

_____

_____

_____

_____

These are ways I might find answers to my questions:

_____

_____

_____

_____

_____

_____

These are books I plan to read:

_____

_____

_____

_____

_____

_____

Here are answers I have found:

_____

_____

_____

_____

_____

_____

_____

These are ways I might present the information I have found:

_____

_____

_____

_____

_____

_____

_____

_____

_____

Learning from an Interview

The other students at Chibi's school did not know him very well. After they learned more about him, they felt differently toward him. Select a classmate or another person at school that you do not know very well. Write some questions that will help you get to know this person better. Then interview the person and write his or her answers below. After the interview, write what you have learned about this person.

1. Question: _____

_____

Answer: _____

_____

2. Question: _____

_____

Answer: _____

_____

3. Question: _____

_____

Answer: _____

_____

What did you learn about the person you interviewed?

_____

_____

Checking Out Facts

Sometimes our fears can make us see a situation differently than it really is. Think of ways that you would use to make sure you are seeing a situation clearly. Write them below.

1. _____
_____
_____
_____

2. _____
_____
_____
_____

3. _____
_____
_____
_____

4. _____
_____
_____
_____

Learning Through Observation

The Greeks learned the earth is round because they observed and asked questions about what they saw.

Find something in nature you have noticed and wondered about. It might be a plant, animal, insect, rock, or something else that has caught your eye. Maybe you have even stopped to look at it. Write below how you would go about learning more about it.

Something interesting I've noticed is: _____

_____

Questions I have about what I've noticed: _____

_____

_____

_____

This is what I would do to learn more about it:

_____

_____

_____

_____

_____

_____

_____

Pretending

Pretending sometimes changes the way things or people appear to others. Sometimes pretending is a fun way to play. Sometimes pretending is a way to trick someone. Think of an example of each kind of pretending. Write your ideas below. Then compare the two examples. What differences do you see between them?

An example of pretending for fun:

_____

_____

_____

An example of pretending in order to trick someone:

_____

_____

_____

Here are some differences between these two kinds of pretending:

1. _____

_____

2. _____

_____

Unit Wrap-up

How did you feel about this unit?

☐ I enjoyed it very much.   ☐ I liked it.

☐ I liked some of it.   ☐ I didn't like it.

How would you rate the difficulty of the unit?

☐ easy   ☐ medium   ☐ hard

How would you rate your performance during this unit?

☐ I learned a lot about appearances.

☐ I learned some things about appearances.

☐ I didn't learn much about appearances.

Why did you choose this rating?

_____

_____

_____

_____

What was the most interesting thing that you learned about appearances?

_____

_____

_____

_____

_____

_____

What did you learn about appearances that you didn't know before?

_____

_____

_____

What did you learn about yourself as a learner?

_____

_____

_____

What do you need to work on as a learner?

_____

_____

_____

What resources (books, films, magazines, interviews, tool cards, other) did you use on your own during this unit? Which of these were the most helpful? Why?

_____

_____

_____

_____

_____

_____

Unit 6/Appearances

Knowledge About Our Country:
The Early Years

This is what I know about the early years of our country before reading the unit.

_____

_____

_____

_____

_____

_____

These are some things I would like to know about the early years of our country.

_____

_____

_____

_____

_____

_____

Reminder: I should read this page again when I get to the end of the unit to see how much I have learned about the early years of our country.

Recording Concept Information

As I read each story, this is what I found out about the early years of our country.

The First Americans by Jane Werner Watson

_____

_____

_____

_____

_____

Follow the Dream by Peter Sis

_____

_____

_____

_____

_____

"Squanto and the First Thanksgiving" by Joyce K. Kessel

_____

_____

_____

_____

_____

Recording Concept Information *continued*

"James Forten: Hero and True Friend" by Carol Siedell

_____

_____

_____

_____

Buttons for General Washington by Peter and Connie Roop

_____

_____

_____

_____

"The First Fourth of July" by Charles P. Graves

_____

_____

_____

_____

The Pioneers by Marie and Douglas Gorsline

_____

_____

_____

_____

Using the Card Catalog

Remember that the title of the book, the author's name, and the subject are listed in alphabetical order in the card catalog.

What subject do you want to find out about?

_____

What letter in the card catalog will you look under to find this subject?

_____

Choose one card that names a book about your subject. What is the author's name?

_____

What is the title of the book?

_____

Is there something on the card that tells where to find the book? Write it here.

_____

Find this book in the library. If you need to, ask the librarian to help you find the right area to look in.

People and Events from Early America

During the early years of our country there were
many important people and events. In your reading
and research for this unit, you will find out more

Person or Event

_____

_____

_____

Why was the person or the event important?

_____

_____

_____

_____

_____

_____

_____

_____

about these people and these events. To keep track of
what you learn, write your ideas in the boxes below.

Person or Event

_____

_____

_____

Why was the person or the event important?

_____

_____

_____

_____

_____

_____

_____

Research Cycle: Problem Phase

A good problem for our group to research:

_____

_____

_____

_____

_____

Why this is an interesting research problem:

_____

_____

_____

_____

_____

_____

Some other questions about this problem:

_____

_____

_____

_____

_____

_____

Research Cycle: Our Idea (or Conjecture) Phase

Our problem:

_____

_____

_____

_____

Conjecture (my first idea or explanation):

_____

_____

_____

_____

_____

_____

_____

_____

_____

_____

As you collect information, your first idea or explanation will change. Return to this page to record your new ideas or explanations about your research problem.

Map of the World

A map of the world is a flat drawing of the world. People use maps to help them find places. You can use this page to find out where people who came to America were from.

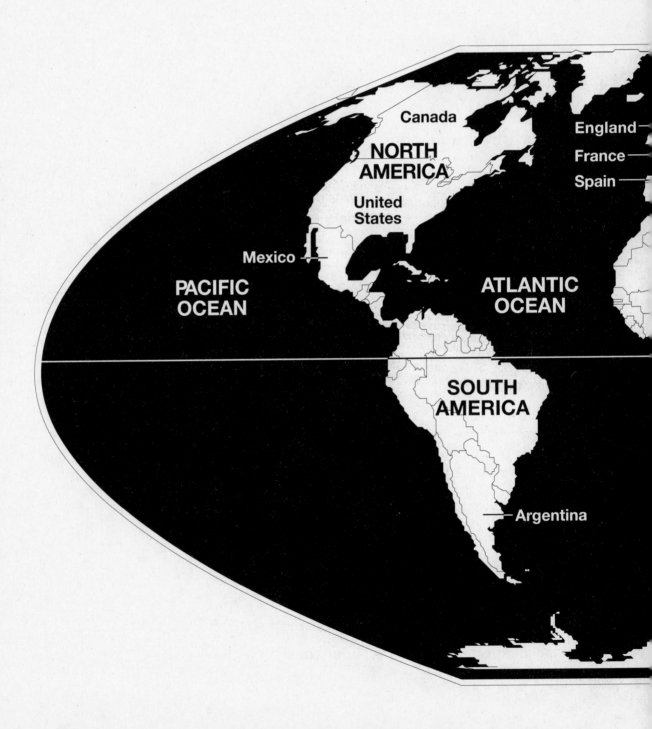

Canada

NORTH AMERICA

England

France

Spain

United States

Mexico

PACIFIC OCEAN

ATLANTIC OCEAN

SOUTH AMERICA

Argentina

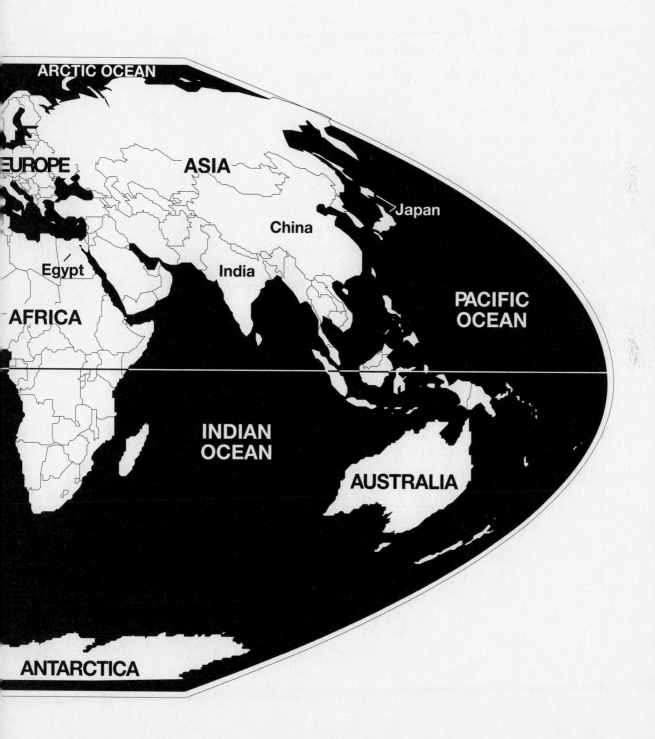

ARCTIC OCEAN

EUROPE

ASIA

Japan

China

Egypt

India

AFRICA

PACIFIC
OCEAN

INDIAN
OCEAN

AUSTRALIA

ANTARCTICA

Taking Notes About the First Thanksgiving

Note-Taking Checklist:

- Make subject headings. Use them to keep the facts you want to remember in order.
- Write down only the most important facts about your research questions or problems.
- Write your notes in your own words.
- Keep your notes short. Use only important words.

Who was at the feast?	
What were the foods people ate?	
How did the people entertain themselves?	

Research Cycle: Needs and Plans Phase

My group's problem:

_____

_____

Knowledge Needs—Information I need to find or figure out in order to help explore the problem:

A. _____

B. _____

C. _____

D. _____

E. _____

Source	Useful?	How?
Encyclopedias		
Books		
Magazines		
Newspapers		
Videotapes, filmstrips, etc.		
Television		
Interviews, observations		
Museums		
Other		

Research Cycle: Group Plan

Our research problem:

_____

_____

_____

Group Members	Main Jobs

Card Catalog

Most libraries keep a card catalog that tells about the books in the library. Here is a sample card for a book about maps and globes:

subject listing:	1. Maps 2. Globes
call number:	JUV BRO 105.B76
author's name:	Ray Broekel
title of book:	Maps and Globes
publisher:	Regensteiner Publishing Enterprises
date of publication:	(c) 1983
number of pages:	45

summary: Briefly discusses different types of maps and globes and explains such map-related terms as symbol, key, directory, and scale.

Remember that the letters *JUV* in the call number are a clue. They tell in what part of the library the book is kept. *JUV* stands for juvenile or children's books.

Using the Card Catalog

Remember that the title of the book, the author's name, and the subject are listed in alphabetical order in the card catalog.

What subject do you want to find out about?

_____

What letter in the card catalog will you look under to find this subject?

_____

Choose one card that names a book about your subject. What is the author's name?

_____

What is the title of the book?

_____

Is there something on the card that tells where to find the book? Write it here.

_____

Find this book in the library. If you need to, ask the librarian to help you find the right area to look in.

Taking Notes

This is a question that I would like to explore about the story *Buttons for General Washington:*

_____

_____

Headings	Notes

Following a Route on a Map: The Oregon Trail

Use the map below to follow the route of the pioneers on their trip west. This route is known as the Oregon Trail. Then write a sentence or two telling what you think was most interesting or important about this route.

This is what I think was most interesting or important about this route:

_____

_____

_____

Following a Route

The Old Spanish Trail was another route used by travelers going west in the 1860s. Study this route from Santa Fe to Los Angeles. Then tell what a trip might have been like for pioneers who used this route.

This is what I think a trip along this route might have been like:

_____

_____

_____

This is how I might use maps during my research or in my research project:

_____

_____

_____

Unit Wrap-up

How did you feel about this unit?

☐ I enjoyed it very much.　　☐ I liked it.

☐ I liked some of it.　　☐ I didn't like it.

How would you rate the difficulty of the unit?

☐ easy　　☐ medium　　☐ hard

How would you rate your performance during this unit?

☐ I learned a lot about the early years of our country.

☐ I learned some new things about the early years of our country.

☐ I didn't learn much about the early years of our country.

Why did you choose this rating?

_____

_____

_____

_____

What was the most interesting thing that you learned about the early years of our country?

_____

_____

_____

_____

_____

What did you learn about the early years of our country that you didn't know before?

_____

_____

_____

What did you learn about yourself as a learner?

_____

_____

_____

What do you need to work on as a learner?

_____

_____

_____

What resources (books, films, magazines, interviews, tool cards, other) did you use on your own during this unit? Which of these were the most helpful? Why?

_____

_____

_____

_____

Knowledge About Our Country:
E Pluribus Unum

This is what I know about the people of our country before reading the unit.

_____

_____

_____

_____

_____

_____

These are some things I would like to know about the people of our country.

_____

_____

_____

_____

_____

_____

   Reminder: I should read this page again when I get
to the end of the unit to see how much I have learned
about the people of our country.

Recording Concept Information

   As I read each story, this is what I found out about the people of our country.

"Out of Many People, One Nation" by Wiley

_____

_____

_____

_____

_____

_____

_____

Abraham Lincoln by David A. Adler

_____

_____

_____

_____

_____

_____

_____

_____

Recording Concept Information *continued*

"Indian Children Long Ago" by Nancy Byrd Turner

_____

_____

_____

_____

_____

"Buffalo Dusk" by Carl Sandburg

_____

_____

_____

_____

_____

"La Florida" by Thekla von Schrader

_____

_____

_____

_____

_____

"East Meets West" by Jennifer Johnson

_____

_____

_____

_____

_____

Watch the Stars Come Out by Rikki Levinson

_____

_____

_____

_____

_____

Martin Luther King, Jr. by David A. Adler

_____

_____

_____

_____

_____

Unit 8/Our Country: *E Pluribus Unum*

One of Many

The talents of many people help make the United States a strong nation. The talents of many people can help any group. Think of a group you belong to. It might be a club, a team, or a school group, such as your class. Explain the purpose of the group. Write how you help the group. Write how others help the group.

This is the name of a group I belong to:

_____

This is the purpose of the group:

_____

_____

_____

This is how I help the group:

_____

_____

_____

This is how others help the group:

_____

_____

_____

Research Cycle: Problem Phase

A good problem for our group to research:

_____

_____

_____

_____

_____

Why this is an interesting research problem:

_____

_____

_____

_____

_____

Some other questions about this problem:

_____

_____

_____

_____

_____

_____

Time-Line Checklist

- Each dot on the time line stands for a date.

- Each line stands for one event.

- Events are listed on the time line from left to right in the order in which they happened. The earliest event is at the far left.

- A time line can be made for any set of events; however, time lines usually show only important events.

How would you use a time line in your research project?

_____

_____

_____

_____

_____

_____

_____

_____

_____

_____

Our Country: *E Pluribus Unum*/Unit 8

Making a Time Line

Fill in the time line below with the following events in the life of George Washington. Write each date and event on the time line. Use another piece of paper if necessary.

1732   Born

1752   Served in Virginia militia

1759   Completed service in the militia

1759   Married Martha Custis

1775   Became commander in chief during Revolutionary War

1783   Retired from the military

1789   Began first term as president

1797   Ended second term as president

1799   Died

Revolutionary War and Civil War

You have read about two important wars during the early years of our country, the Revolutionary War and the Civil War. Write down one of the causes of each war. Then write down one way in which our country changed after each war.

One cause for the Revolutionary War:

_____

_____

_____

One way the United States changed after this war:

_____

_____

_____

One cause for the Civil War:

_____

_____

_____

One way the United States changed after this war:

_____

_____

_____

Research Cycle: Our Idea (or Conjecture) Phase

Our problem:

_____

_____

_____

_____

_____

Conjecture (my first idea or explanation):

_____

_____

_____

_____

_____

_____

_____

_____

_____

    As you collect information, your first idea or explanation will change. Return to this page to record new ideas or explanations about your research problem.

Thinking About Explorers

Ponce de León and Columbus were important explorers in early American history. There are explorers today, too. People explore oceans, space, rain forests, and many other places. Write your ideas about explorers on this page.

Why I think explorers are important:

_____

_____

_____

These are some dangers explorers face:

_____

_____

_____

Why I think people want to explore:

_____

_____

_____

What kind of person makes a good explorer:

_____

_____

_____

Finding Sources

It is important to know where to find the information you need for your research. Use this page to write the best sources for finding information. Explain your reasons for using a source.

Research question: _____

_____

A good source of information is _____

_____

I would use this source because _____

_____

I can find this source _____

_____

Another good source of information is _____

_____

I would use this source because _____

_____

I can find this source _____

_____

If necessary, ask the librarian to help you find the area where your source is located.

Research Cycle: Needs and Plans Phase

My group's problem:

_____

_____

_____

Knowledge Needs—Information I need to find or figure out in order to help explore the problem:

A. _____

B. _____

C. _____

D. _____

E. _____

Source	Useful?	How?
Encyclopedias		
Books		
Magazines		
Newspapers		
Videotapes, filmstrips, etc.		
Television		
Interviews, observations		
Museums		
Other		

Research Cycle: Group Plan

Our research problem:

_____

_____

_____

_____

_____

Group Members	Main Jobs

Out of Many People, One Nation

You have read about and talked about the many different groups of people who make up our country. In the chart below, list facts that you have learned and shared about our different groups.

Group	Holidays or Feasts	Foods

Group	Holidays or Feasts	Foods

A Special Trip

Moving from one place to another, or from one country to another, can make us feel excited or sad or even frightened. How would you feel if you were on a trip to begin a new life in the United States? Think of the trips you have read about in the units about the early years and the people of our country. Imagine yourself on a trip you might like to take. Then write a letter to someone you left behind, telling about your feelings and experiences. Share the letter with a classmate or classmates.

Dear _____

_____

_____

_____

_____

_____

_____

_____

_____

_____

Making Changes: A Voice in How Things Are Done

Martin Luther King, Jr., did not like the way that African-American people were treated. He spoke up about these problems and did things that led to changes in the lives of African Americans. In our country, each person can do something to bring about change.

Think of a problem that you care about. It could be in your school, in your community, or in the country. Write the problem. Then write what you think could be done to correct this problem. Talk about your ideas with your classmates.

Problem:

_____

_____

_____

Here are some ways to correct the problem:

_____

_____

_____

_____

Unit Wrap-up

How did you feel about this unit?

☐ I enjoyed it very much.　　☐ I liked it.

☐ I liked some of it.　　☐ I didn't like it.

How would you rate the difficulty of the unit?

☐ easy　　☐ medium　　☐ hard

How would you rate your performance during this unit?

☐ I learned a lot about the people of our country.

☐ I learned some things about the people of our country.

☐ I didn't learn much about the people of our country.

Why did you choose this rating?

_____

_____

_____

_____

What was the most interesting thing that you learned about the people of our country?

_____

_____

_____

_____

_____

What did you learn about the people of our country that you didn't know before?

_____

_____

_____

What did you learn about yourself as a learner?

_____

_____

_____

What do you need to work on as a learner?

_____

_____

_____

What resources (books, films, magazines, interviews, tool cards, other) did you use on your own during this unit? Which of these were the most helpful? Why?

_____

_____

_____

_____

_____

The Research Cycle

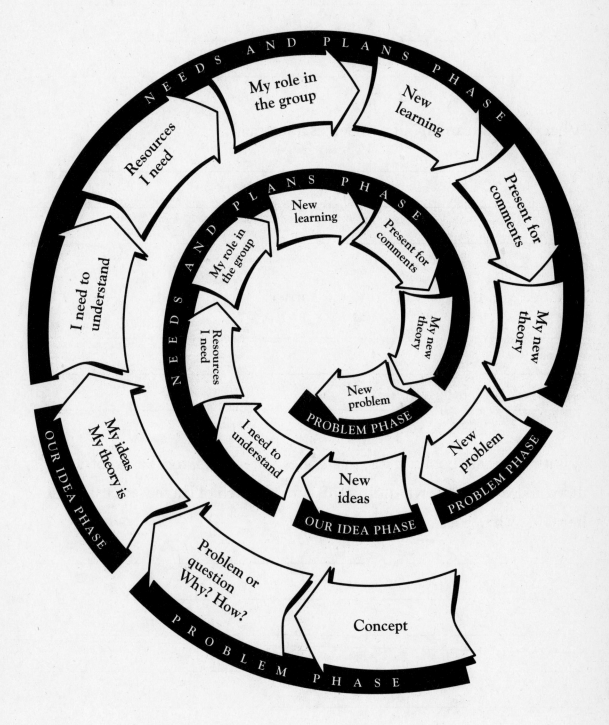